LAST NIGHT, THE MOU~

Manuela Moser's poetry has ~~appe~~
Ireland Review, *Partisan Hotel*, *The Tangerine*, and *The Forward Book of Poetry 2021*. She runs The Lifeboat Press, and is a co-Director at Catalyst Arts.

Last night, the mountain

Published by Bad Betty Press in 2021
www.badbettypress.com

Cover design by Amy Acre

Printed and bound in the United Kingdom

A CIP record of this book is available from the British Library.

ISBN: 978-1-913268-22-0

Supported using public funding by
**ARTS COUNCIL
ENGLAND**

LOTTERY FUNDED

Last night, the mountain

BAD BETTY PRESS

Last night,
the mountain

Contents

One of your responsibilities is to think of yourself as alone

—Another: to query the war there are too many to choose from

—To understand as a character the fabric of it

—To have a privileged relationship with language

Most of what you understand is wrong

—You cannot say 'this is a simple thing'

—Complex things resurrect the ordinary and you must

To give a character something she cannot escape is a 'cosmic injustice'

We were in America, we were on a trip and yet we were home and
by home I mean that the bathroom was familiar

I recognised the green tiled walls and the dark wooden cabinet, I
remembered moving the cabinet from our old home into this one

And there was a bar serving iced tea but you had to ask for lemon or
wine if you preferred and almost everyone was there and I went to
wake you

Because we were late but someone was watching you sleep and they
said you weren't late at all so I went out into the snow

And thought about running the goodwill store because the owner of
the bar said it would be a good career move

And when was it we heard the deer being shot?

Strange that at the time we couldn't have known it was a deer—

Only by seeing it, dead, slung over a shoulder, did we understand—

And yet, every time I replay it in my memory, the sound of the shot ringing out—

Unmistakably a deer, glimpsed through trees, upright and then not

This bit happens all too quickly, you say the word, then you're flying
ten feet up in the air and I scream at you

that you are the most birdlike creature I've ever seen, and then all of
a sudden I'm up there too and I reach out

And we tumble to earth. You started to forgive me right that second
but I've never let you forget how it felt and of course I blame myself

Years later we've developed greater powers and I'm trying to teach
you a lesson so I put your hands and your feet into concrete

But by the time I've told you to break free the concrete has hardened
and this for some reason causes your oesophagus to close

And you're speechless, soon your eyes glaze over, you're in a
swimming pool but it's pointless and sad

Let's say this place was all whites, and greys, and blues

And we walked up the stairs,

      And it's peculiar now, how I knew it

All of those signs

      And it was purely received—recent knowledge

From another place quite like this but smaller perhaps, with fewer windows; stairs

We are back in the same familiar place and my brother has turned
from a tiger into a boy for the first time ever and we play with a ball
of string

The forests are damp with mist and I am watching birds dive into
the mudded sand to find worms and they're chirruping and yes that
sound

Down there on the beach is someone skipping over the rocks and
when I look it's him, the mist is heavier

And he is more like a tiger than ever before and yet completely a boy
with knee high socks on, a child all at once

And what were we here for anyway? What had we come to find
because it's not here and neither is the ocean

All of Prague felt like ghosts to me, you say

And so I went to Prague and it was cold and it was beautiful because it was cold and I got used to the feeling

Each morning I threw open the windows to watch the swans on the river while you were sitting on the deck of a beach house somewhere in Maine watching sailboats and drinking tea

Back then my dreams were actually enjoyable

Now I'm thinking about what he said about monotheism, deserts, God as creator—perfect, transcendent, etc—

And sand and mountains and houses on the side of mountains, the bushes that grow there and sun and that barbwire fence

No clouds, no breeze, no water, what I mean is the heat

The heat in the desert that doesn't fall with the sun; that makes the scent of rosemary good up to a heavy point; that burns like sleet when you first feel it

For example, in nothing is tenderness as important as here

I dreamt that I sent you a poem and you replied 'you're an amateur
you're gorgeous' and then we swapped sex tapes

except of course I stole mine off the internet and it wasn't a sex tape
but a collage full of people

and someone had a finger in someone else's mouth and I was on the
train to Dublin I was on the train to somewhere

and there were my siblings all of a blur and we sat down wearing
white Victorian blouses because that's the style

and its pebble-dashed, it's the solstice and how nice to be young and
able to steal a sex tape and how shocked I was

to see you even if it was only in my dream on the way to Dublin or
not on the way to Dublin I'm not sure

I swam 40 lengths in the pool today

In the next lane over there were five people, carefully manoeuvring a woman's body onto a yellow piece of plastic the length of a body

Each time I swam from the deep end to the shallow I watched their progress

How many straps they had clipped around her

How carefully they lifted her onto the tiled side of the pool

It was good for me, I concentrated on their movements

Soon she was unstrapped and they were loading the next body onto the bright yellow plastic

This time there was a tornado or at least the wind and rain were
exceedingly heavy and they sent a helicopter because someone was
sick

But it couldn't land, and anyway I couldn't decide which coat to wear
and you were in a wine bar unaware of most of this

Later that week we met at the memorial, the sky was blue and
cloudy and my niece chased her dog up flights of winding staircases

And nearly fell but somehow was fine even though the experience of
watching had left me shattered/floored/unable to respond/catch her

Upon each it is a pattern of logic or of purpose

   —If this bewilders inward, it is neither nerves nor outrage

      —For what it's worth, it quakes, it quickens

Recall the patterns

   —And aren't you tired with listening yet?

      —It's all there is, if you can bear it

As though I don't deserve to live with such beauty, you say:

   —The summer was both glorious and chaotic

      —I was by the sea, I woke up early to the heavy sounds of water

We were sketching and I've never been very good at it, letting the
lines shape the image rather than the thing itself in front of me

The deal was I'd bathe my feet in the stream but never jump the
whole way in and you'd leave me alone

For the whole of eternity but it's never that easy and by the time I'd
finished my sketch

Of the forest and the concrete and the sky you'd gone and I laughed
but more so I cried or at least I tried to

It has been posited by some that you can never have enough time to
capture it all

> —And yet by more that it's at least worth trying to
> get at what's left

Could you ever write yourself out, tell a story that isn't about yourself?

> —And yet to suggest that you could make yourself a constant
> in a landscape is presuming too much, is absurd at best:

Now I doubt I could even open my eyes to it

> —And yet I attempt it, in the never ending water falling always
> upwards through the blue

The moon swinging down like a pendulum happened to be the
central thing in the universe

And we were right there when it began, in a remote mountain
village looking up at the sky

There were too many constellations and a bright comet of light that
many when asked about afterwards found erotic

And there were seven lakes and when I looked up again at the sky
I couldn't see even one of the drawings and that in itself seemed a
shame

The trees are moving

Sometimes they move together and sometimes they move apart

The church bells are ringing

You can hear the storm beyond the mountain

The sounds of water are too fluid/varied/rushing/it's more than silence

We walk to one lake and then the next

There are tadpoles, we catch them wriggling in our palms

Up here it's wrong to talk about the rush of water

The golden rusted sunlight on the mountain

How long after you've woken can you tell it's raining?

You've honed your style or the seasons

Somewhere there is light and the windows are open and only the smallest of sounds can come in

Last night the mountain looked like crushed velvet against the sky

We stood on the balcony and we looked at the moon and the moon was right there above the mountain in a pool of light

*

Now it is morning the mountain pronounces

The cowbells ring and ring and my dad calls *hello! hello!* and the blue flowers on the balcony have closed to the cold

In the garden the stream rushes down and it is cool in the shade

We follow streams home

We are waiting for the weather to change

A taxi driver points to a rook in the sky and says *Here, when we see a dark bird like this, we expect snow. That's Basho* you whisper

I am here where the stream sounds and the ground is covered in alpine strawberries and animals crawl in the shadows

*

The tops of my feet feel like ice

Today is the first day we have not seen the mountain

Trees and beyond the fir trees only white

Nothing again, the white bleeding into white

I can hear the stream now the rain has stopped

There are spider threads stretching between the branches in the sunlight and the wind

I've never understood what they mean when they say it lingers somewhere in the mind like toothache

The words sitting in the periphery of my mind when I wake up at five when I wake up at seven

Fuck, my dad says, *fuck it*, over and over, slamming his palm on the table between the boiled eggs, cups of coffee, cherry jam and braided challah

Sometimes I think that as the cloud draws closer, the mountain comes clearer into view

On the train to Chur we pass over the viaduct

I see streams, tributaries

This morning there is snow on the mountain

This morning the mountain has already disappeared

For example, this happens more often than you may think

We were circled round low tables listening and that was about the
height of it

Earlier we'd found stone engravings, climbed over marble ledges and
rocks covered in moss to read them when really they meant nothing
to us

I wanted to play in the carnival but every time I went to find an
instrument the music/water had evaporated

Making it impossible and anyway we were on a flight, the doors
opened and we were still moving

And the air hostesses said that's it, breath it in and we all filled our
lungs with the dark blue ink of the sky

Before the plane took off again and that was all folks nothing special
here

Right there in the park at 5pm the sun is still shining but not like
before

Everywhere is green and yellow and I am screaming vulgarity

I want those delaying months back where I lay beneath the grey sky

Where only the softness of white crocus swept under me

Acknowledgements

For their advice and support in the writing of these poems, my
thanks go to Stephen Connolly, Susannah Dickey, Leontia Flynn,
Dane Holt, Zosia Kuczyńska, Tara McEvoy, Scott McKendry,
Padraig Regan, and all my friends at the Seamus Heaney Centre,
Queen's University, Belfast. My thanks also to Amy Acre and Jake
Wild Hall at Bad Betty Press. Acknowledgments and thanks are due
to the editors at *Partisan Hotel*, *The Stinging Fly* and *The Tangerine*,
where some of these poems first appeared. Thanks to Ciaran Carson,
Mary Denvir, and my family.

Lightning Source UK Ltd.
Milton Keynes UK
UKHW010028141221
395594UK00002B/158

9 781913 268220